50 Delicious Barbecue Dishes

By: Kelly Johnson

Table of Contents

- Pulled Pork Sandwiches
- Baby Back Ribs
- Brisket
- Grilled Chicken Wings
- BBQ Chicken
- Grilled Sausages
- Beef Short Ribs
- BBQ Pulled Chicken
- Grilled Corn on the Cob
- Smoked Salmon
- Grilled Shrimp Skewers
- Burnt Ends
- Barbecue Meatballs
- Grilled Steak
- Grilled Veggie Skewers
- Smoked Turkey
- BBQ Pork Ribs

- Grilled Lamb Chops
- Grilled Fish Tacos
- Smoked Brisket Sandwiches
- BBQ Pulled Jackfruit
- Grilled Asparagus with BBQ Sauce
- Grilled Portobello Mushrooms
- BBQ Beef Sliders
- Grilled Pineapple
- Smoked Chicken Thighs
- BBQ Baked Beans
- Grilled Peppers and Onions
- Barbecue Pork Belly
- Grilled Flatbreads
- BBQ Tofu Skewers
- Grilled Squash
- Barbecue Meatloaf
- Smoked Sausages
- BBQ Tri-Tip
- Grilled Caesar Salad

- Grilled Tomatoes with Basil
- BBQ Chicken Tenders
- Grilled Sweet Potatoes
- Pulled Beef Brisket Sandwiches
- BBQ Shrimp Po' Boy
- Grilled Stuffed Peppers
- Smoked Lamb Shoulder
- BBQ Chicken Legs
- Grilled Eggplant
- Grilled Potato Wedges
- BBQ Shrimp and Grits
- Grilled Bacon-Wrapped Asparagus
- Smoked Fish Fillets
- Grilled Lemon Herb Chicken

Pulled Pork Sandwiches

Ingredients:

- 3 lbs pork shoulder
- 1 tbsp paprika
- 1 tbsp brown sugar
- 1 tbsp salt
- 1 tsp black pepper
- 1 tsp garlic powder
- 1 tsp onion powder
- 1/2 tsp cayenne pepper
- 1/2 cup apple cider vinegar
- 1/2 cup BBQ sauce
- 8 hamburger buns
- Coleslaw (optional, for serving)

Instructions:

1. Preheat your oven to 300°F (150°C).
2. Mix paprika, brown sugar, salt, pepper, garlic powder, onion powder, and cayenne pepper in a bowl. Rub the mixture all over the pork shoulder.
3. Place the pork shoulder in a roasting pan, cover with foil, and roast for 4-5 hours, or until the pork is tender and easily shreds.

4. Once cooked, remove from the oven and shred the pork with two forks.

5. Mix the shredded pork with apple cider vinegar and BBQ sauce.

6. Serve on hamburger buns with coleslaw, if desired.

Baby Back Ribs

Ingredients:

- 2 racks baby back ribs
- 1/4 cup brown sugar
- 2 tbsp paprika
- 1 tbsp salt
- 1 tbsp black pepper
- 1 tsp chili powder
- 1 tsp garlic powder
- 1 tsp onion powder
- 1/2 tsp cayenne pepper
- 1 cup BBQ sauce

Instructions:

1. Preheat the oven to 275°F (135°C).
2. Mix brown sugar, paprika, salt, pepper, chili powder, garlic powder, onion powder, and cayenne pepper in a small bowl.
3. Remove the thin membrane from the ribs and rub the spice mixture all over the ribs.
4. Place the ribs on a baking sheet, cover with foil, and bake for 2.5-3 hours.
5. Preheat the grill to medium heat.

6. Remove the ribs from the oven, brush with BBQ sauce, and grill for 5-10 minutes until the sauce is caramelized.

7. Slice and serve hot.

Brisket

Ingredients:

- 5-6 lbs beef brisket
- 2 tbsp kosher salt
- 1 tbsp black pepper
- 1 tbsp paprika
- 1 tbsp garlic powder
- 1 tsp onion powder
- 1 tsp cumin
- 1/2 cup beef broth
- 1/4 cup BBQ sauce (optional)

Instructions:

1. Preheat the oven to 300°F (150°C).
2. Mix salt, pepper, paprika, garlic powder, onion powder, and cumin in a bowl. Rub the spice mixture all over the brisket.
3. Place the brisket in a roasting pan, fat side up. Pour the beef broth into the pan.
4. Cover the pan tightly with foil and bake for 3-4 hours, until the brisket is tender.
5. Optionally, brush with BBQ sauce and broil for an additional 5 minutes for a caramelized finish.
6. Slice against the grain and serve.

Grilled Chicken Wings

Ingredients:

- 2 lbs chicken wings
- 2 tbsp olive oil
- 1 tbsp paprika
- 1 tbsp garlic powder
- 1 tsp onion powder
- Salt and pepper, to taste
- BBQ sauce or buffalo sauce, for dipping

Instructions:

1. Preheat the grill to medium heat.
2. Toss the chicken wings with olive oil, paprika, garlic powder, onion powder, salt, and pepper.
3. Grill the wings for 20-25 minutes, turning occasionally, until they are golden brown and cooked through.
4. Serve with your favorite dipping sauce.

BBQ Chicken

Ingredients:

- 4 bone-in, skin-on chicken breasts
- 1/4 cup olive oil
- 1/4 cup apple cider vinegar
- 1/4 cup BBQ sauce
- Salt and pepper, to taste

Instructions:

1. Preheat the grill to medium heat.
2. In a small bowl, mix olive oil, apple cider vinegar, BBQ sauce, salt, and pepper.
3. Brush the chicken breasts with the BBQ mixture.
4. Grill the chicken for 6-8 minutes per side, until cooked through and juices run clear.
5. Serve hot with additional BBQ sauce, if desired.

Grilled Sausages

Ingredients:

- 4 sausages of your choice
- 1 tbsp olive oil
- 1 onion, sliced
- 1 bell pepper, sliced

Instructions:

1. Preheat the grill to medium heat.
2. Grill the sausages for 10-12 minutes, turning occasionally, until they are cooked through and have grill marks.
3. Meanwhile, heat olive oil in a skillet over medium heat and sauté the onions and bell peppers until softened, about 5-7 minutes.
4. Serve the sausages with the sautéed onions and peppers.

Beef Short Ribs

Ingredients:

- 4 beef short ribs
- 1 tbsp olive oil
- 2 tbsp brown sugar
- 1 tbsp paprika
- 1 tbsp garlic powder
- 1 tsp cumin
- 1/2 cup beef broth
- 1/2 cup BBQ sauce

Instructions:

1. Preheat the oven to 325°F (165°C).
2. Heat olive oil in a skillet over medium-high heat. Brown the short ribs on all sides, about 4-5 minutes.
3. In a small bowl, mix brown sugar, paprika, garlic powder, and cumin. Rub the spice mixture over the ribs.
4. Place the ribs in a roasting pan, pour the beef broth around them, cover with foil, and bake for 2.5-3 hours.
5. Brush with BBQ sauce and broil for 5 minutes to caramelize the sauce.
6. Serve hot.

BBQ Pulled Chicken

Ingredients:

- 4 chicken breasts
- 1 tbsp olive oil
- 1/2 cup BBQ sauce
- 1/4 cup apple cider vinegar
- 1 tbsp honey
- 8 buns for serving

Instructions:

1. Preheat the oven to 350°F (175°C).
2. Heat olive oil in a skillet over medium heat. Add chicken breasts and cook for 6-8 minutes per side until golden.
3. In a small bowl, combine BBQ sauce, apple cider vinegar, and honey.
4. Pour the sauce over the chicken and bake for 20-25 minutes until the chicken is cooked through.
5. Shred the chicken with two forks and mix it with the sauce.
6. Serve on buns with extra BBQ sauce.

Grilled Corn on the Cob

Ingredients:

- 4 ears of corn, husked
- 2 tbsp butter
- Salt and pepper, to taste

Instructions:

1. Preheat the grill to medium-high heat.
2. Grill the corn for 10-12 minutes, turning occasionally until the kernels are lightly charred.
3. Brush with butter and season with salt and pepper. Serve hot.

Smoked Salmon

Ingredients:

- 2 lbs fresh salmon fillets
- 1/4 cup brown sugar
- 1/4 cup salt
- 1 tbsp black pepper
- 1/2 cup maple syrup
- 2 tbsp lemon juice

Instructions:

1. Mix brown sugar, salt, and pepper in a bowl. Rub the mixture onto the salmon fillets.
2. Let the salmon sit in the refrigerator for 2 hours to marinate.
3. Preheat the smoker to 225°F (110°C).
4. Smoke the salmon for 1.5-2 hours, or until the fish flakes easily with a fork.
5. Brush with maple syrup and lemon juice before serving.

Grilled Shrimp Skewers

Ingredients:

- 1 lb large shrimp, peeled and deveined
- 2 tbsp olive oil
- 2 tbsp lemon juice
- 2 garlic cloves, minced
- 1 tbsp chopped fresh parsley
- Salt and pepper, to taste
- Wooden skewers (soaked in water for 30 minutes)

Instructions:

1. Preheat the grill to medium-high heat.
2. In a bowl, mix olive oil, lemon juice, garlic, parsley, salt, and pepper.
3. Thread the shrimp onto the soaked skewers.
4. Brush the shrimp with the marinade and grill for 2-3 minutes per side, until opaque and cooked through.
5. Serve with extra lemon wedges and fresh herbs.

Burnt Ends

Ingredients:

- 4 lbs beef brisket, cut into 2-inch cubes
- 1/4 cup olive oil
- 2 tbsp brown sugar
- 2 tbsp paprika
- 1 tbsp black pepper
- 1 tbsp garlic powder
- 1 tbsp onion powder
- 1 tsp cayenne pepper
- 1/2 cup BBQ sauce

Instructions:

1. Preheat the smoker or grill to 250°F (120°C).
2. Mix brown sugar, paprika, black pepper, garlic powder, onion powder, cayenne, and salt in a bowl.
3. Rub the brisket cubes with olive oil, then coat them with the seasoning mixture.
4. Smoke the cubes for 3-4 hours, or until they are tender.
5. Toss the burnt ends with BBQ sauce and return them to the smoker or grill for an additional 30 minutes to caramelize.
6. Serve hot.

Barbecue Meatballs

Ingredients:

- 1 lb ground beef
- 1/2 cup breadcrumbs
- 1/4 cup grated Parmesan cheese
- 1 egg
- 2 garlic cloves, minced
- 1/4 cup chopped parsley
- 1/2 cup BBQ sauce

Instructions:

1. Preheat the grill to medium heat.
2. In a bowl, mix ground beef, breadcrumbs, Parmesan, egg, garlic, parsley, salt, and pepper.
3. Form the mixture into 1-inch meatballs.
4. Grill the meatballs for 8-10 minutes, turning occasionally, until cooked through.
5. Brush with BBQ sauce during the last 2 minutes of grilling.
6. Serve with extra BBQ sauce on the side.

Grilled Steak

Ingredients:

- 2 ribeye or sirloin steaks
- 2 tbsp olive oil
- 1 tbsp garlic powder
- 1 tbsp onion powder
- 1 tsp dried thyme
- Salt and pepper, to taste

Instructions:

1. Preheat the grill to high heat.
2. Rub the steaks with olive oil and season with garlic powder, onion powder, thyme, salt, and pepper.
3. Grill the steaks for 4-6 minutes per side for medium-rare, or adjust based on desired doneness.
4. Let the steaks rest for 5 minutes before slicing and serving.

Grilled Veggie Skewers

Ingredients:

- 1 zucchini, sliced
- 1 bell pepper, cut into chunks
- 1 red onion, cut into wedges
- 1 cup cherry tomatoes
- 1 cup mushrooms, halved
- 2 tbsp olive oil
- 1 tbsp balsamic vinegar
- 1 tbsp dried oregano
- Salt and pepper, to taste
- Wooden skewers (soaked in water for 30 minutes)

Instructions:

1. Preheat the grill to medium heat.
2. Thread the vegetables onto the soaked skewers.
3. In a small bowl, mix olive oil, balsamic vinegar, oregano, salt, and pepper.
4. Brush the veggies with the marinade and grill for 5-7 minutes, turning occasionally, until tender and charred.
5. Serve immediately.

Smoked Turkey

Ingredients:

- 1 whole turkey (10-12 lbs)
- 1/4 cup olive oil
- 1 tbsp dried thyme
- 1 tbsp garlic powder
- 1 tbsp onion powder
- 1 tsp paprika
- Salt and pepper, to taste
- 1/2 cup apple cider (for basting)

Instructions:

1. Preheat the smoker to 225°F (110°C).
2. Rub the turkey inside and out with olive oil and season with thyme, garlic powder, onion powder, paprika, salt, and pepper.
3. Smoke the turkey for 6-8 hours, or until the internal temperature reaches 165°F (75°C) in the thickest part of the breast.
4. Baste with apple cider every 1-2 hours to keep the turkey moist.
5. Let the turkey rest for 15 minutes before carving.

BBQ Pork Ribs

Ingredients:

- 2 racks pork ribs
- 2 tbsp paprika
- 1 tbsp garlic powder
- 1 tbsp brown sugar
- 1 tsp salt
- 1 tsp black pepper
- 1/2 tsp cayenne pepper
- 1 cup BBQ sauce

Instructions:

1. Preheat the grill to medium-low heat.
2. Rub the ribs with paprika, garlic powder, brown sugar, salt, black pepper, and cayenne.
3. Place the ribs on the grill and cook for 2-3 hours, turning occasionally, until tender.
4. Brush with BBQ sauce during the last 30 minutes of grilling.
5. Slice and serve with additional BBQ sauce.

Grilled Lamb Chops

Ingredients:

- 8 lamb chops
- 2 tbsp olive oil
- 2 tbsp fresh rosemary, chopped
- 2 garlic cloves, minced
- 1 tsp lemon zest
- Salt and pepper, to taste

Instructions:

1. Preheat the grill to medium-high heat.
2. In a small bowl, mix olive oil, rosemary, garlic, lemon zest, salt, and pepper.
3. Rub the mixture over the lamb chops and let them marinate for 30 minutes.
4. Grill the lamb chops for 3-4 minutes per side for medium-rare, or adjust based on desired doneness.
5. Serve hot.

Grilled Fish Tacos

Ingredients:

- 1 lb white fish fillets (like tilapia or cod)
- 2 tbsp olive oil
- 1 tbsp lime juice
- 1 tsp chili powder
- Salt and pepper, to taste
- 8 small flour tortillas
- 1/2 cup cabbage slaw
- 1/4 cup fresh cilantro, chopped
- Lime wedges

Instructions:

1. Preheat the grill to medium heat.
2. Brush the fish fillets with olive oil, lime juice, chili powder, salt, and pepper.
3. Grill the fish for 3-4 minutes per side, or until it flakes easily with a fork.
4. Warm the tortillas on the grill for 1-2 minutes.
5. Assemble the tacos by placing the grilled fish on the tortillas, topping with cabbage slaw, cilantro, and lime wedges.
6. Serve immediately.

Smoked Brisket Sandwiches

Ingredients:

- 2 lbs smoked brisket, sliced
- 8 sandwich rolls
- 1/2 cup BBQ sauce
- Pickles (optional)

Instructions:

1. Preheat the grill to medium-low heat.
2. Slice the smoked brisket into thin slices.
3. Toast the sandwich rolls on the grill for 1-2 minutes.
4. Layer the sliced brisket on the rolls and drizzle with BBQ sauce.
5. Top with pickles if desired and serve hot.

BBQ Pulled Jackfruit

Ingredients:

- 2 cans young green jackfruit in brine, drained and shredded
- 1 tbsp olive oil
- 1 onion, chopped
- 2 garlic cloves, minced
- 1 cup BBQ sauce
- 1 tbsp apple cider vinegar
- 1 tsp smoked paprika
- Salt and pepper, to taste
- Buns (for serving)

Instructions:

1. In a large pan, heat olive oil over medium heat.
2. Add the onion and garlic, cooking until softened, about 5 minutes.
3. Add the shredded jackfruit, BBQ sauce, apple cider vinegar, smoked paprika, salt, and pepper. Stir to combine.
4. Cover and cook on low heat for 30-40 minutes, stirring occasionally, until the jackfruit has absorbed the flavors.
5. Serve the pulled jackfruit on buns with extra BBQ sauce and your favorite slaw.

Grilled Asparagus with BBQ Sauce

Ingredients:

- 1 lb fresh asparagus, trimmed
- 2 tbsp olive oil
- Salt and pepper, to taste
- 1/4 cup BBQ sauce

Instructions:

1. Preheat the grill to medium-high heat.
2. Toss the asparagus with olive oil, salt, and pepper.
3. Grill the asparagus for 4-5 minutes, turning occasionally, until tender and lightly charred.
4. Brush the asparagus with BBQ sauce during the last minute of grilling.
5. Serve immediately with extra BBQ sauce on the side.

Grilled Portobello Mushrooms

Ingredients:

- 4 large portobello mushroom caps
- 2 tbsp olive oil
- 1 tbsp balsamic vinegar
- 2 garlic cloves, minced
- 1 tsp dried thyme
- Salt and pepper, to taste

Instructions:

1. Preheat the grill to medium-high heat.
2. In a small bowl, combine olive oil, balsamic vinegar, garlic, thyme, salt, and pepper.
3. Brush the mushroom caps with the marinade and let them sit for 10 minutes.
4. Grill the mushrooms for 4-5 minutes per side, until tender and grill marks appear.
5. Serve as a main dish or on a bun as a burger alternative.

BBQ Beef Sliders

Ingredients:

- 1 lb ground beef
- 1/4 cup breadcrumbs
- 1/4 cup BBQ sauce
- 1 tsp garlic powder
- 1/2 tsp onion powder
- Salt and pepper, to taste
- 8 slider buns
- Additional BBQ sauce for serving

Instructions:

1. Preheat the grill to medium-high heat.
2. In a bowl, combine ground beef, breadcrumbs, BBQ sauce, garlic powder, onion powder, salt, and pepper.
3. Form the mixture into 8 small patties.
4. Grill the patties for 3-4 minutes per side, or until they reach your desired doneness.
5. Place the patties on slider buns and drizzle with additional BBQ sauce.
6. Serve with pickles or slaw, if desired.

Grilled Pineapple

Ingredients:

- 1 ripe pineapple, peeled, cored, and sliced into rings
- 2 tbsp honey
- 1 tbsp lime juice
- 1/2 tsp cinnamon

Instructions:

1. Preheat the grill to medium-high heat.
2. In a small bowl, whisk together honey, lime juice, and cinnamon.
3. Brush the pineapple rings with the honey mixture.
4. Grill the pineapple for 3-4 minutes per side, until caramelized and grill marks appear.
5. Serve as a side dish or dessert.

Smoked Chicken Thighs

Ingredients:

- 4 bone-in, skin-on chicken thighs
- 2 tbsp olive oil
- 1 tbsp paprika
- 1 tsp garlic powder
- 1 tsp onion powder
- Salt and pepper, to taste
- Wood chips for smoking

Instructions:

1. Preheat the smoker to 250°F (120°C), adding wood chips for flavor.
2. Rub the chicken thighs with olive oil, paprika, garlic powder, onion powder, salt, and pepper.
3. Place the chicken thighs in the smoker and cook for 2-3 hours, or until the internal temperature reaches 165°F (75°C).
4. Let the chicken rest for 5 minutes before serving.

BBQ Baked Beans

Ingredients:

- 2 cans baked beans
- 1/4 cup BBQ sauce
- 1/4 cup brown sugar
- 1/2 onion, chopped
- 2 tbsp mustard
- 1 tbsp apple cider vinegar
- 1/2 tsp smoked paprika

Instructions:

1. Preheat the grill to medium heat.
2. In a large pan, combine baked beans, BBQ sauce, brown sugar, onion, mustard, apple cider vinegar, and smoked paprika.
3. Place the pan on the grill and cook for 30-40 minutes, stirring occasionally, until bubbly and heated through.
4. Serve hot.

Grilled Peppers and Onions

Ingredients:

- 2 bell peppers, cut into strips
- 1 onion, cut into wedges
- 2 tbsp olive oil
- Salt and pepper, to taste

Instructions:

1. Preheat the grill to medium-high heat.
2. Toss the peppers and onions with olive oil, salt, and pepper.
3. Grill the veggies for 4-5 minutes per side, until charred and tender.
4. Serve as a side dish or topping for burgers.

Barbecue Pork Belly

Ingredients:

- 2 lbs pork belly, cut into strips
- 1/4 cup soy sauce
- 2 tbsp brown sugar
- 2 tbsp apple cider vinegar
- 1 tbsp garlic powder
- 1 tsp smoked paprika
- Salt and pepper, to taste

Instructions:

1. Preheat the grill to medium-high heat.
2. In a bowl, mix soy sauce, brown sugar, apple cider vinegar, garlic powder, smoked paprika, salt, and pepper.
3. Marinate the pork belly strips in the mixture for at least 30 minutes.
4. Grill the pork belly strips for 4-5 minutes per side, until crispy and caramelized.
5. Serve as a main dish or in sandwiches.

Grilled Flatbreads

Ingredients:

- 2 cups all-purpose flour
- 1 tsp salt
- 1 tbsp olive oil
- 1/2 cup warm water
- 1 tsp yeast
- 1 tsp sugar
- 1 tbsp olive oil (for brushing)

Instructions:

1. In a bowl, combine warm water, yeast, and sugar. Let sit for 5 minutes to activate.
2. In a large mixing bowl, combine flour, salt, and olive oil. Add the yeast mixture and stir until a dough forms.
3. Knead the dough on a floured surface for 5-7 minutes, then let it rest in a greased bowl for 1 hour.
4. Preheat the grill to medium-high heat.
5. Divide the dough into 4 portions and roll each portion into a flatbread shape.
6. Brush the flatbreads with olive oil and grill for 2-3 minutes per side until golden and slightly crispy.
7. Serve with your favorite toppings or dips.

BBQ Tofu Skewers

Ingredients:

- 1 block firm tofu, pressed and cut into cubes
- 1/4 cup BBQ sauce
- 1 tbsp olive oil
- 1 tbsp soy sauce
- 1 tsp smoked paprika
- 1 tbsp lemon juice
- Salt and pepper, to taste
- Skewers (wooden or metal)

Instructions:

1. Preheat the grill to medium heat.
2. In a bowl, combine BBQ sauce, olive oil, soy sauce, smoked paprika, lemon juice, salt, and pepper.
3. Thread the tofu cubes onto the skewers.
4. Brush the tofu with the BBQ sauce mixture and let marinate for at least 15 minutes.
5. Grill the skewers for 4-5 minutes per side, brushing with more BBQ sauce as they cook.
6. Serve hot with extra BBQ sauce on the side.

Grilled Squash

Ingredients:

- 2 medium zucchinis, sliced into 1/2-inch rounds
- 2 medium yellow squash, sliced into 1/2-inch rounds
- 2 tbsp olive oil
- 1 tsp garlic powder
- 1 tsp dried thyme
- Salt and pepper, to taste

Instructions:

1. Preheat the grill to medium-high heat.
2. Toss the zucchini and yellow squash slices with olive oil, garlic powder, thyme, salt, and pepper.
3. Grill the squash for 3-4 minutes per side until lightly charred and tender.
4. Serve immediately as a side dish.

Barbecue Meatloaf

Ingredients:

- 1 lb ground beef
- 1/2 lb ground pork
- 1 cup breadcrumbs
- 1/2 cup BBQ sauce, plus extra for topping
- 1/4 cup milk
- 1 egg
- 1 onion, finely chopped
- 2 garlic cloves, minced
- 1 tsp dried oregano
- Salt and pepper, to taste

Instructions:

1. Preheat the grill to medium heat and set it up for indirect grilling.
2. In a large bowl, combine ground beef, ground pork, breadcrumbs, BBQ sauce, milk, egg, onion, garlic, oregano, salt, and pepper.
3. Form the mixture into a loaf shape and place it on a grill-safe tray or pan.
4. Grill the meatloaf for about 45 minutes, basting with BBQ sauce every 15 minutes.
5. Check for doneness (internal temperature should be 160°F).
6. Let rest for 10 minutes before slicing. Serve with extra BBQ sauce.

Smoked Sausages

Ingredients:

- 4 sausages (bratwurst, Italian, or your favorite variety)
- 1 tbsp olive oil
- 1 tsp paprika
- Salt and pepper, to taste
- Wood chips for smoking (optional)

Instructions:

1. Preheat the smoker to 225°F (107°C) and add wood chips for smoking.
2. Rub the sausages with olive oil, paprika, salt, and pepper.
3. Place the sausages in the smoker and cook for 1.5-2 hours, or until fully cooked through.
4. Serve with your favorite condiments and sides.

BBQ Tri-Tip

Ingredients:

- 2-3 lb tri-tip roast
- 2 tbsp olive oil
- 1 tbsp garlic powder
- 1 tbsp onion powder
- 1 tsp paprika
- 1 tsp ground cumin
- Salt and pepper, to taste
- 1/4 cup BBQ sauce

Instructions:

1. Preheat the grill to medium-high heat, setting up for indirect grilling.
2. In a bowl, combine olive oil, garlic powder, onion powder, paprika, cumin, salt, and pepper.
3. Rub the tri-tip with the spice mixture and let sit for 15 minutes.
4. Grill the tri-tip on indirect heat for about 25-30 minutes, flipping once.
5. During the last 5 minutes of grilling, brush with BBQ sauce and continue grilling until the internal temperature reaches 135°F for medium-rare.
6. Let the meat rest for 10 minutes before slicing.

Grilled Caesar Salad

Ingredients:

- 2 Romaine lettuce hearts, halved
- 1 tbsp olive oil
- Salt and pepper, to taste
- 1/2 cup Caesar dressing
- 1/4 cup grated Parmesan cheese
- Croutons (optional)

Instructions:

1. Preheat the grill to medium-high heat.
2. Brush the cut sides of the romaine lettuce with olive oil and season with salt and pepper.
3. Grill the lettuce halves, cut side down, for about 2-3 minutes until charred but still crisp.
4. Drizzle with Caesar dressing, sprinkle with Parmesan, and top with croutons if desired.
5. Serve immediately as a unique side or appetizer.

Grilled Tomatoes with Basil

Ingredients:

- 4 large tomatoes, halved
- 2 tbsp olive oil
- 1/2 tsp garlic powder
- Salt and pepper, to taste
- Fresh basil leaves, for garnish

Instructions:

1. Preheat the grill to medium-high heat.
2. Brush the cut sides of the tomatoes with olive oil and sprinkle with garlic powder, salt, and pepper.
3. Grill the tomatoes cut side down for 2-3 minutes until lightly charred.
4. Garnish with fresh basil leaves and serve warm as a side dish or topping.

BBQ Chicken Tenders

Ingredients:

- 1 lb chicken tenders
- 1/4 cup BBQ sauce
- 1 tbsp olive oil
- Salt and pepper, to taste

Instructions:

1. Preheat the grill to medium heat.
2. Brush the chicken tenders with olive oil and season with salt and pepper.
3. Grill the chicken for 3-4 minutes per side, basting with BBQ sauce during the last minute of grilling.
4. Check the internal temperature (should be 165°F) before serving.

Grilled Sweet Potatoes

Ingredients:

- 2 large sweet potatoes, sliced into rounds
- 2 tbsp olive oil
- 1 tsp ground cinnamon
- Salt and pepper, to taste

Instructions:

1. Preheat the grill to medium-high heat.
2. Toss the sweet potato slices with olive oil, cinnamon, salt, and pepper.
3. Grill the sweet potatoes for 3-4 minutes per side until tender and grill marks appear.
4. Serve immediately as a sweet side dish.

Pulled Beef Brisket Sandwiches

Ingredients:

- 3-4 lb beef brisket
- 1 tbsp olive oil
- 1 tbsp paprika
- 1 tbsp garlic powder
- 1 tsp onion powder
- Salt and pepper, to taste
- 1 cup BBQ sauce
- Soft sandwich buns

Instructions:

1. Preheat the grill to medium-low heat for indirect grilling.
2. Rub the brisket with olive oil, paprika, garlic powder, onion powder, salt, and pepper.
3. Grill the brisket for about 4-5 hours, turning occasionally, until tender.
4. Shred the brisket with a fork and mix with BBQ sauce.
5. Serve on sandwich buns with extra BBQ sauce.

BBQ Shrimp Po' Boy

Ingredients:

- 1 lb large shrimp, peeled and deveined
- 1/4 cup BBQ sauce
- 4 soft hoagie rolls
- 1/2 cup shredded lettuce
- 1/2 cup sliced tomatoes
- 1/4 cup sliced pickles
- 1/4 cup mayonnaise
- 1 tbsp lemon juice
- 1 tsp hot sauce (optional)
- Salt and pepper, to taste

Instructions:

1. Preheat the grill to medium heat.
2. Toss the shrimp with BBQ sauce and season with salt and pepper.
3. Grill the shrimp for 2-3 minutes per side until fully cooked.
4. In a small bowl, mix the mayonnaise, lemon juice, and hot sauce (if using).
5. Toast the hoagie rolls on the grill for 1-2 minutes.
6. Spread the mayo mixture on both sides of the rolls.
7. Layer the shredded lettuce, tomatoes, pickles, and grilled shrimp on the rolls.
8. Serve the Po' Boy with extra hot sauce if desired.

Grilled Stuffed Peppers

Ingredients:

- 4 bell peppers, tops cut off and seeds removed
- 1 lb ground turkey or beef
- 1 cup cooked rice
- 1 can diced tomatoes (14.5 oz), drained
- 1 small onion, finely chopped
- 2 cloves garlic, minced
- 1 tsp ground cumin
- 1 tsp paprika
- 1/2 tsp chili powder
- Salt and pepper, to taste
- 1 cup shredded cheese (cheddar, mozzarella, or your choice)

Instructions:

1. Preheat the grill to medium heat.
2. In a skillet, sauté the onion and garlic with olive oil until softened.
3. Add the ground turkey or beef and cook until browned.
4. Stir in the rice, diced tomatoes, cumin, paprika, chili powder, salt, and pepper.
5. Stuff the bell peppers with the mixture and top with shredded cheese.
6. Wrap each stuffed pepper in foil and place on the grill.
7. Grill for 20-25 minutes, flipping halfway through, until the peppers are tender and the filling is hot.

8. Serve with a side salad or grilled vegetables.

Smoked Lamb Shoulder

Ingredients:

- 4-5 lb lamb shoulder
- 2 tbsp olive oil
- 1 tbsp garlic powder
- 1 tbsp rosemary, finely chopped
- 1 tsp thyme
- Salt and pepper, to taste
- 1/2 cup white wine or broth (for basting)

Instructions:

1. Preheat your smoker to 250°F (121°C).
2. Rub the lamb shoulder with olive oil and season with garlic powder, rosemary, thyme, salt, and pepper.
3. Place the lamb shoulder in the smoker and smoke for 4-5 hours, or until the internal temperature reaches 190°F for fall-apart tenderness.
4. Baste the lamb with white wine or broth every hour to keep it moist.
5. Remove the lamb from the smoker and let it rest for 15 minutes.
6. Shred the lamb and serve with your favorite sides.

BBQ Chicken Legs

Ingredients:

- 10-12 chicken legs (drumsticks)
- 1/4 cup BBQ sauce
- 1 tbsp olive oil
- 1 tbsp paprika
- 1 tsp garlic powder
- 1 tsp onion powder
- 1/2 tsp smoked paprika (optional)
- Salt and pepper, to taste

Instructions:

1. Preheat the grill to medium heat.
2. In a small bowl, mix olive oil, paprika, garlic powder, onion powder, smoked paprika, salt, and pepper.
3. Rub the chicken legs with the seasoning mixture.
4. Grill the chicken legs for 25-30 minutes, turning occasionally, until the internal temperature reaches 165°F.
5. During the last 5 minutes of grilling, brush the chicken legs with BBQ sauce.
6. Serve the BBQ chicken legs with extra sauce on the side.

Grilled Eggplant

Ingredients:

- 2 medium eggplants, sliced into 1/2-inch thick rounds
- 3 tbsp olive oil
- 1 tbsp balsamic vinegar
- 2 cloves garlic, minced
- Salt and pepper, to taste
- Fresh herbs (parsley, basil, or thyme), for garnish

Instructions:

1. Preheat the grill to medium heat.
2. In a small bowl, mix the olive oil, balsamic vinegar, minced garlic, salt, and pepper.
3. Brush both sides of the eggplant slices with the oil mixture.
4. Grill the eggplant for 3-4 minutes per side until tender and lightly charred.
5. Garnish with fresh herbs and serve as a side or appetizer.

Grilled Potato Wedges

Ingredients:

- 4 medium potatoes, cut into wedges
- 3 tbsp olive oil
- 1 tsp garlic powder
- 1 tsp paprika
- Salt and pepper, to taste
- Fresh parsley, for garnish

Instructions:

1. Preheat the grill to medium-high heat.
2. In a large bowl, toss the potato wedges with olive oil, garlic powder, paprika, salt, and pepper.
3. Arrange the wedges on the grill and cook for 15-20 minutes, turning occasionally, until golden and crispy.
4. Remove from the grill and garnish with fresh parsley. Serve as a side dish.

BBQ Shrimp and Grits

Ingredients:

- 1 lb large shrimp, peeled and deveined
- 2 tbsp olive oil
- 1 tbsp BBQ seasoning
- 1 cup grits
- 2 cups water or chicken broth
- 1/2 cup heavy cream
- 2 tbsp butter
- 1/2 cup shredded cheddar cheese
- Salt and pepper, to taste
- Fresh parsley, for garnish

Instructions:

1. Cook the grits according to package instructions, using water or chicken broth for extra flavor. Stir in the heavy cream, butter, and cheese once cooked. Season with salt and pepper.
2. While the grits cook, preheat the grill to medium-high heat. Toss the shrimp with olive oil and BBQ seasoning.
3. Grill the shrimp for 2-3 minutes per side until they turn pink and opaque.
4. Serve the BBQ shrimp over a bed of creamy grits, garnished with fresh parsley.

Grilled Bacon-Wrapped Asparagus

Ingredients:

- 1 bunch asparagus, trimmed
- 8 slices of bacon
- Olive oil, for drizzling
- Salt and pepper, to taste
- Fresh lemon wedges, for serving

Instructions:

1. Preheat the grill to medium heat.
2. Wrap each asparagus spear with a slice of bacon, securing the ends with toothpicks.
3. Lightly drizzle the bacon-wrapped asparagus with olive oil and season with salt and pepper.
4. Grill for 6-8 minutes, turning occasionally, until the bacon is crispy and the asparagus is tender.
5. Serve with a squeeze of fresh lemon juice.

Smoked Fish Fillets

Ingredients:

- 2 fish fillets (salmon, trout, or white fish)
- 2 tbsp olive oil
- 1 tbsp lemon juice
- 1 tsp smoked paprika
- 1 tsp garlic powder
- Salt and pepper, to taste
- Wood chips for smoking

Instructions:

1. Preheat your smoker to 225°F (107°C).
2. Rub the fish fillets with olive oil, lemon juice, smoked paprika, garlic powder, salt, and pepper.
3. Place the fish fillets on the smoker grate, skin-side down.
4. Smoke the fish for 1-2 hours until the internal temperature reaches 145°F.
5. Serve with fresh lemon wedges or your favorite dipping sauce.

Grilled Lemon Herb Chicken

Ingredients:

- 4 boneless, skinless chicken breasts
- 3 tbsp olive oil
- 2 tbsp lemon juice
- 2 cloves garlic, minced
- 1 tbsp fresh thyme, chopped
- 1 tbsp fresh rosemary, chopped
- Salt and pepper, to taste

Instructions:

1. Preheat the grill to medium-high heat.
2. In a bowl, whisk together the olive oil, lemon juice, garlic, thyme, rosemary, salt, and pepper.
3. Coat the chicken breasts with the marinade and let sit for 20-30 minutes.
4. Grill the chicken for 6-7 minutes per side, or until the internal temperature reaches 165°F.
5. Let the chicken rest for a few minutes before serving.

www.ingramcontent.com/pod-product-compliance
Lightning Source LLC
LaVergne TN
LVHW081322060526
838201LV00055B/2399